ONE HUNDRED POEMS FRO...
...HE CHINESE

中國詩百首

Also by Kenneth Rexroth

published by New Directions

ONE HUNDRED POEMS
FROM THE CHINESE

by

KENNETH REXROTH

A NEW DIRECTIONS BOOK

The decorative calligraphy of the names of the poets in this volume is by Wango Wêng, to whom the publisher and translator are grateful.

Library of Congress Catalog Card Number: 56-13351.
Clothbound (ISBN: 0-81120370-0)
New Directions Paperbook 192 (ISBN: 0-8112-0180-5)
Published in Canada by Penguin Books Canada Limited
New Directions Books are published for James Laughlin by New Directions Publishing Corporation,
80 Eighth Avenue, New York 10011

Manufactured in the United States
New Directions Books are printed on acid-free paper

TWENTY-THIRD PRINTING

TABLE OF CONTENTS

INTRODUCTION

This book is in two parts. First there are thirty-five poems by Tu Fu. They are based on the text in the Harvard Yenching Concordance to Tu Fu, of which one volume gives the poems themselves. I have taken note of William Hung's prose translations, of Florence Ayscough's literal renderings, and of the German of Erwin von Zach. Over the years I have had many discussions of the poems and my translations with Chinese friends, none of them specialists, notably my friend, C. H. Kwock. However, these translations are my own. In some cases they are very free, in others as exact as possible, depending on how I felt in relation to the particular poem at the time. The freer ones are usually those done long ago. I have had the work of Tu Fu by me since adolescence and over the years have come to know these poems better than most of my own.

The second part is a selection of poetry of the Sung Dynasty, most of it never in English before. Here, where I did not have a Chinese text at hand in the first place, for about half the poems, I usually translated from other Western languages, mostly the French of Soulié de Morant and G. Margouliès. Both of these translations have considerable merit as poetry in their own right. Later I took my translations to the originals and changed them around to suit myself. Again, what has resulted is my own responsibility, sometimes more literal, more often freer, than the Tu Fu renderings. I hope in all cases they are true to the spirit of the originals, and valid English poems.

I might say that Sung poetry, so much less compact than that of T'ang, Tu Fu's period, permits more liberties. There is no special reason for this procedure —I just happened to have a number of European versions of Sung poetry and a few texts at hand the last two summers in the mountains, and was able to finish up in libraries in the winter. And, I was anxious to get a good selection of the vast mass of Sung poetry, not anthologized satisfactorily even in Chinese, into English. The whole spirit of this time in China is very congenial today, especially to the romantic, empirical-mystic and antinomian taste which has prevailed in the arts of the West since 1940. Not only does Sung poetry deserve to be better known, but it includes one of China's very greatest poets, Su Tung P'o, and Li Ch'ing Chao, her greatest poetess. Perhaps, someday, when I have more time to spend in the libraries of university Oriental departments, I will do "100 Poems of Sung" and "100 Poems of Tu Fu." So, here are two selections of poetry, one the work of a couple of years, the other the personal distillate of a lifetime. I hope they meet the somewhat different ends I have in view. I make no claim for the book as a piece of Oriental scholarship. Just some poems.

K. R.

TU FU

BANQUET AT THE TSO FAMILY MANOR

The windy forest is checkered
By the light of the setting,
Waning moon. I tune the lute,
Its strings are moist with dew.
The brook flows in the darkness
Below the flower path. The thatched
Roof is crowned with constellations.
As we write the candles burn short.
Our wits grow sharp as swords while
The wine goes round. When the poem
Contest is ended, someone
Sings a song of the South. And
I think of my little boat,
And long to be on my way.

TU FU

WRITTEN ON THE WALL AT CHANG'S HERMITAGE

It is Spring in the mountains.
I come alone seeking you.
The sound of chopping wood echos
Between the silent peaks.
The streams are still icy.
There is snow on the trail.
At sunset I reach your grove
In the stony mountain pass.
You want nothing, although at night
You can see the aura of gold
And silver ore all around you.
You have learned to be gentle
As the mountain deer you have tamed.
The way back forgotten, hidden
Away, I become like you,
An empty boat, floating, adrift.

TU FU

WINTER DAWN

The men and beasts of the zodiac
Have marched over us once more.
Green wine bottles and red lobster shells,
Both emptied, litter the table.
"Should auld acquaintance be forgot?" Each
Sits listening to his own thoughts,
And the sound of cars starting outside.
The birds in the eaves are restless,
Because of the noise and light. Soon now
In the winter dawn I will face
My fortieth year. Borne headlong
Towards the long shadows of sunset
By the headstrong, stubborn moments,
Life whirls past like drunken wildfire.

TU FU

IV

SNOW STORM

Tumult, weeping, many new ghosts.
Heartbroken, aging, alone, I sing
To myself. Ragged mist settles
In the spreading dusk. Snow skurries
In the coiling wind. The wineglass
Is spilled. The bottle is empty.
The fire has gone out in the stove.
Everywhere men speak in whispers.
I brood on the uselessness of letters.

TU FU

VISITING TSAN, ABBOT OF TA-YUN

I am sleepless in the glow and shadow of the lamplight.
The heart at peace breathes the incense of dedication.
Between the temple walls the night is bottomless.
The gold wind bells quiver in the breeze.
The courtyard shuts in the deep
Darkness of the Spring night.
In the blackness the crystalline pool
Exhales the perfume of flowers.
The Northern Crown crosses the sky
Cut by the temple roof,
Where an iron phoenix soars and twists in the air.
The chanting of prayers floats from the hall.
Fading bell notes eddy by my bed.
Tomorrow in the sunlight
I shall walk in the manured fields,
And weep for the yellow dust of the dead.

TU FU

MOON FESTIVAL

The Autumn constellations
Begin to rise. The brilliant
Moonlight shines on the crowds.
The moon toad swims in the river
And does not drown. The moon rabbit
Pounds the bitter herbs of the
Elixir of eternal life.
His drug only makes my heart
More bitter. The silver brilliance
Only makes my hair more white.
I know that the country is
Overrun with war. The moonlight
Means nothing to the soldiers
Camped in the western deserts.

TU FU

JADE FLOWER PALACE

The stream swirls. The wind moans in
The pines. Grey rats scurry over
Broken tiles. What prince, long ago,
Built this palace, standing in
Ruins beside the cliffs? There are
Green ghost fires in the black rooms.
The shattered pavements are all
Washed away. Ten thousand organ
Pipes whistle and roar. The storm
Scatters the red autumn leaves.
His dancing girls are yellow dust.
Their painted cheeks have crumbled
Away. His gold chariots
And courtiers are gone. Only
A stone horse is left of his
Glory. I sit on the grass and
Start a poem, but the pathos of
It overcomes me. The future
Slips imperceptibly away.
Who can say what the years will bring?

TU FU

VIII

TRAVELLING NORTHWARD

Screech owls moan in the yellowing
Mulberry trees. Field mice scurry,
Preparing their holes for winter.
Midnight, we cross an old battlefield.
The moonlight shines cold on white bones.

TU FU

IX

WAITING FOR AUDIENCE ON A SPRING NIGHT

The flowers along the palace
Walls grow dim in the twilight.
Twittering birds fly past to roost.
Twinkling stars move over ten
Thousand households. The full moon
Enters the Ninth Constellation.
Wakeful, I hear the rattle
Of gold keys in locks. I hear jade
Bridle pendants tinkling in
The wind. At the dawn audience
I must present a special
Memorial. Time and again
I wonder how long the night will last.

TU FU

TO WEI PA, A RETIRED SCHOLAR

The lives of many men are
Shorter than the years since we have
Seen each other. Aldebaran
And Antares move as we have.
And now, what night is this? We sit
Here together in the candle
Light. How much longer will our prime
Last? Our temples are already
Grey. I visit my old friends.
Half of them have become ghosts.
Fear and sorrow choke me and burn
My bowels. I never dreamed I would
Come this way, after twenty years,
A wayfarer to your parlor.
When we parted years ago,
You were unmarried. Now you have
A row of boys and girls, who smile
And ask me about my travels.
How have I reached this time and place?
Before I can come to the end
Of an endless tale, the children
Have brought out the wine. We go
Out in the night and cut young
Onions in the rainy darkness.
We eat them with hot, steaming,
Yellow millet. You say, "It is
Sad, meeting each other again."

We drink ten toasts rapidly from
The rhinoceros horn cups.
Ten cups, and still we are not drunk.
We still love each other as
We did when we were schoolboys.
Tomorrow morning mountain peaks
Will come between us, and with them
The endless, oblivious
Business of the world.

TU FU

BY THE WINDING RIVER I

Every day on the way home from
My office I pawn another
Of my Spring clothes. Every day
I come home from the river bank
Drunk. Everywhere I go, I owe
Money for wine. History
Records few men who lived to be
Seventy. I watch the yellow
Butterflies drink deep of the
Flowers, and the dragonflies
Dipping the surface of the
Water again and again.
I cry out to the Spring wind,
And the light and the passing hours.
We enjoy life such a little
While, why should men cross each other?

TU FU

BY THE WINDING RIVER II

Everywhere petals are flying
And Spring is fading. Ten thousand
Atoms of sorrow whirl away
In the wind. I will watch the last
Flowers as they fade, and ease
The pain in my heart with wine.
Two kingfishers mate and nest in
The ruined river pavilion.
Stone unicorns, male and female,
Guard the great tomb near the park.
After the laws of their being,
All creatures pursue happiness.
Why have I let an official
Career swerve me from my goal?

TU FU

XIII

TO PI SSU YAO

We have talent. People call us
The leading poets of our day.
Too bad, our homes are humble,
Our recognition trivial.
Hungry, ill clothed, servants treat
Us with contempt. In the prime
Of life, our faces are wrinkled.
Who cares about either of us,
Or our troubles? We are our own
Audience. We appreciate
Each other's literary
Merits. Our poems will be handed
Down along with great dead poets'.
We can console each other.
At least we shall have descendants.

TU FU

XIV

LONELINESS

A hawk hovers in air.
Two white gulls float on the stream.
Soaring with the wind, it is easy
To drop and seize
Birds who foolishly drift with the current.
Where the dew sparkles in the grass,
The spider's web waits for its prey.
The processes of nature resemble the business of men.
I stand alone with ten thousand sorrows.

TU FU

XV

CLEAR AFTER RAIN

Autumn, cloud blades on the horizon.
The west wind blows from ten thousand miles.
Dawn, in the clear morning air,
Farmers busy after long rain.
The desert trees shed their few green leaves.
The mountain pears are tiny but ripe.
A Tartar flute plays by the city gate.
A single wild goose climbs into the void.

TU FU

XVI

NEW MOON

The bright, thin, new moon appears,
Tipped askew in the heavens.
It no sooner shines over
The ruined fortress than the
Evening clouds overwhelm it.
The Milky Way shines unchanging
Over the freezing mountains
Of the border. White frost covers
The garden. The chrysanthemums
Clot and freeze in the night.

TU FU

XVII

OVERLOOKING THE DESERT

Clear Autumn. I gaze out into
Endless spaces. The horizon
Wavers in bands of haze. Far off
The river flows into the sky.
The lone city is blurred with smoke.
The wind blows the last leaves away.
The hills grow dim as the sun sets.
A single crane flies late to roost.
The twilit trees are full of crows.

TU FU

XVIII

VISITORS

I have had asthma for a
Long time. It seems to improve
Here in this house by the river.
It is quiet too. No crowds
Bother me. I am brighter
And more rested. I am happy here.
When someone calls at my thatched hut
My son brings me my straw hat
And I go out and gather
A handful of fresh vegetables.
It isn't much to offer.
But it is given in friendship.

TU FU

COUNTRY COTTAGE

A peasant's shack beside the
Clear river, the rustic gate
Opens on a deserted road.
Weeds grow over the public well.
I loaf in my old clothes. Willow
Branches sway. Flowering trees
Perfume the air. The sun sets
Behind a flock of cormorants,
Drying their black wings along the pier.

TU FU

XX

THE WILLOW

My neighbor's willow sways its frail
Branches, graceful as a girl of
Fifteen. I am sad because this
Morning the violent
Wind broke its longest bough.

TU FU

XXI

SUNSET

Sunset glitters on the beads
Of the curtains. Spring flowers
Bloom in the valley. The gardens
Along the river are filled
With perfume. Smoke of cooking
Fires drifts over the slow barges.
Sparrows hop and tumble in
The branches. Whirling insects
Swarm in the air. Who discovered
That one cup of thick wine
Will dispel a thousand cares?

TU FU

FAREWELL ONCE MORE
TO MY FRIEND YEN AT FENG CHI STATION

Here we part.
You go off in the distance,
And once more the forested mountains
Are empty, unfriendly.
What holiday will see us
Drunk together again?
Last night we walked
Arm in arm in the moonlight,
Singing sentimental ballads
Along the banks of the river.
Your honor outlasts three emperors.
I go back to my lonely house by the river,
Mute, friendless, feeding the crumbling years.

TU FU

XXIII

A RESTLESS NIGHT IN CAMP

In the penetrating damp
I sleep under the bamboos,
Under the penetrating
Moonlight in the wilderness.
The thick dew turns to fine mist.
One by one the stars go out.
Only the fireflies are left.
Birds cry over the water.
War breeds its consequences.
It is useless to worry,
Wakeful while the long night goes.

TU FU

XXIV

SOUTH WIND

The days grow long, the mountains
Beautiful. The south wind blows
Over blossoming meadows.
Newly arrived swallows dart
Over the steaming marshes.
Ducks in pairs drowse on the warm sand.

TU FU

XXV

ANOTHER SPRING

White birds over the grey river.
Scarlet flowers on the green hills.
I watch the Spring go by and wonder
If I shall ever return home.

TU FU

XXVI

I PASS THE NIGHT AT GENERAL HEADQUARTERS

A clear night in harvest time.
In the courtyard at headquarters
The wu-tung trees grow cold.
In the city by the river
I wake alone by a guttering
Candle. All night long bugle
Calls disturb my thoughts. The splendor
Of the moonlight floods the sky.
Who bothers to look at it?
Whirlwinds of dust, I cannot write.
The frontier pass is unguarded.
It is dangerous to travel.
Ten years wandering, sick at heart.
I perch here like a bird on a
Twig, thankful for a moment's peace.

TU FU

FAR UP THE RIVER

A pair of golden orioles
Sings in the bright green willows.
A line of white egrets crosses
The clear blue sky. The window
Frames the western mountains, white
With the snows of a thousand years.
Anchored to the pilings are
Boats from eastern Wu,
Three thousand miles from home.

TU FU

CLEAR EVENING AFTER RAIN

The sun sinks towards the horizon.
The light clouds are blown away.
A rainbow shines on the river.
The last raindrops spatter the rocks.
Cranes and herons soar in the sky.
Fat bears feed along the banks.
I wait here for the west wind
And enjoy the crescent moon
Shining through misty bamboos.

TU FU

FULL MOON

Isolate and full, the moon
Floats over the house by the river.
Into the night the cold water rushes away below the gate.
The bright gold spilled on the river is never still.
The brilliance of my quilt is greater than precious silk.
The circle without blemish.
The empty mountains without sound.
The moon hangs in the vacant, wide constellations.
Pine cones drop in the old garden.
The senna trees bloom.
The same clear glory extends for ten thousand miles.

TU FU

NIGHT IN THE HOUSE BY THE RIVER

It is late in the year;
Yin and Yang struggle
In the brief sunlight.
On the desert mountains
Frost and snow
Gleam in the freezing night.
Past midnight,
Drums and bugles ring out,
Violent, cutting the heart.
Over the Triple Gorge the Milky Way
Pulsates between the stars.
The bitter cries of thousands of households
Can be heard above the noise of battle.
Everywhere the workers sing wild songs.
The great heroes and generals of old time
Are yellow dust forever now.
Such are the affairs of men.
Poetry and letters
Persist in silence and solitude.

TU FU

DAWN OVER THE MOUNTAINS

The city is silent,
Sound drains away,
Buildings vanish in the light of dawn,
Cold sunlight comes on the highest peak,
The thick dust of night
Clings to the hills,
The earth opens,
The river boats are vague,
The still sky—
The sound of falling leaves.
A huge doe comes to the garden gate,
Lost from the herd,
Seeking its fellows.

TU FU

HOMECOMING—LATE AT NIGHT

Nightfall. I return from a
Journey along the Tigers'
Trail. The mountains are black.
Everybody is at home
Asleep. The Great Bear descends
To the river. Overhead
The stars are huge in the sky.
When I light the lamps at my
Door, a frightened gibbon cries
Out in the ravine. I hear
The whitehaired watchman on his
Round calling out the hour.
Stick in hand, he keeps
Guard and all is safe.

                              TU FU

XXXIII

STARS AND MOON ON THE RIVER

The Autumn night is clear
After the thunderstorm.
Venus glows on the river.
The Milky Way is white as snow.
The dark sky is vast and deep.
The Northern Crown sets in the dusk.
The moon like a clear mirror
Rises from the great void. When it
Has climbed high in the sky, moonlit
Frost glitters on the chrysanthemums.

TU FU

NIGHT THOUGHTS WHILE TRAVELLING

A light breeze rustles the reeds
Along the river banks. The
Mast of my lonely boat soars
Into the night. Stars blossom
Over the vast desert of
Waters. Moonlight flows on the
Surging river. My poems have
Made me famous but I grow
Old, ill and tired, blown hither
And yon; I am like a gull
Lost between heaven and earth.

TU FU

XXXV

BRIMMING WATER

Under my feet the moon
Glides along the river.
Near midnight, a gusty lantern
Shines in the heart of night.
Along the sandbars flocks
Of white egrets roost,
Each one clenched like a fist.
In the wake of my barge
The fish leap, cut the water,
And dive and splash.

TU FU

MEI YAO CH'EN

XXXVI

AN EXCUSE FOR NOT RETURNING THE VISIT
OF A FRIEND

Do not be offended because
I am slow to go out. You know
Me too well for that. On my lap
I hold my little girl. At my
Knees stands my handsome little son.
One has just begun to talk.
The other chatters without
Stopping. They hang on my clothes
And follow my every step.
I can't get any farther
Than the door. I am afraid
I will never make it to your house.

MEI YAO CH'EN

XXXVII

NEXT DOOR

My neighbors on the right
Have a young son who has just
Commenced to step out.
My neighbors on the left
Have a young daughter
Who is still a virgin.
In the heavy shadow
Under the gate it is very dark
After the sun has set.
Whose head is that, looking over the wall?

MEI YAO CH'EN

XXXVIII

MELON GIRL

The girl who sells melons beside the stream
Gathers her melons in the fields on the hillsides.
She does not need to spin hemp.
She has handsfull of bronze money.

MEI YAO CH'EN

XXXIX

FISH PEDDLER

The fish man chats with the passers by,
As he peddles his perches and breams.
Knife in hand, he scrapes off their scales.
He stamps and swears because their fins are so long.

MEI YAO CH'EN

XL

THE CRESCENT MOON

The crescent moon shines
Over the corner of my house.
My neighbor's dogs howl.
The family is in trouble.
In the middle of the night
Spirits fly about and strange creatures stir.
A murmur runs over the high grass
Although no wind blows.

MEI YAO CH'EN

XLI

ON THE DEATH OF A NEW BORN CHILD

The flowers in bud on the trees
Are pure like this dead child.
The East wind will not let them last.
It will blow them into blossom,
And at last into the earth.
It is the same with this beautiful life
Which was so dear to me.
While his mother is weeping tears of blood,
Her breasts are still filling with milk.

MEI YAO CH'EN

XLII

SORROW

Heaven took my wife. Now it
Has also taken my son.
My eyes are not allowed a
Dry season. It is too much
For my heart. I long for death.
When the rain falls and enters
The earth, when a pearl drops into
The depth of the sea, you can
Dive in the sea and find the
Pearl, you can dig in the earth
And find the water. But no one
Has ever come back from the
Underground Springs. Once gone, life
Is over for good. My chest
Tightens against me. I have
No one to turn to. Nothing,
Not even a shadow in a mirror.

MEI YAO CH'EN

XLIII

A DREAM AT NIGHT

In broad daylight I dream I
Am with her. At night I dream
She is still at my side. She
Carries her kit of colored
Threads. I see her image bent
Over her bag of silks. She
Mends and alters my clothes and
Worries for fear I might look
Worn and ragged. Dead, she watches
Over my life. Her constant
Memory draws me towards death.

MEI YAO CH'EN

XLIV

I REMEMBER THE BLUE RIVER

The moon has a halo, there will be wind.
The boatmen talk together in the night.
Dawn, a brisk wind fills our sail.
We leave the bank and speed over the white waves.
It is no use for me to be here in the land of Wu.
My dream and my desire are back in Ch'ou.
I dreamt that one day she would come with me
On a trip like this, and now she is only dust.

MEI YAO CH'EN

XLV

ON THE DEATH OF HIS WIFE

Since we were first married
Seventeen years have past.
Suddenly I looked up and she was gone.
She said she would never leave me.
My temples are turning white.
What have I to grow old for now?
At death we will be together in the tomb.
Now I am still alive,
And my tears flow without end.

MEI YAO CH'EN

XLVI

IN BROAD DAYLIGHT I DREAM
OF MY DEAD WIFE

Who says that the dead do not think of us?
Whenever I travel, she goes with me.
She was uneasy when I was on a journey.
She always wanted to accompany me.
While I dream, everything is as it used to be.
When I wake up, I am stabbed with sorrow.
The living are often parted and never meet again.
The dead are together as pure souls.

MEI YAO CH'EN

I REMEMBER THE RIVER AT WU SUNG

I remember once, on a journey to the west,
An evening at the mouth of the river, at Wu Sung.
Along the banks a fresh breeze blew against the current.
The pale moon rose between two willow trees.
A single night bird flew far away.
Fishing boats wandered on the river.
And who was with me then?
I weep and think of my dead wife.

MEI YAO CH'EN

XLVIII

A FRIEND ADVISES ME TO STOP DRINKING

In my young days I drank a
Lot of wine. There is nothing
Wrong with the love of drink. Now
I am old and my teeth and
Hairs are few and far between.
I still love to drink, but I
Can't do it like I used to.
Now when I drink it upsets
My stomach. There is not much
Pleasure in it. Today I
Got drunk and could not hold up
My head. The room turned round and round.
Seeking pleasure, I find only
Sickness. This is certainly
Not the way to care for my health.
Maybe I should give it up
Altogether. I am afraid
People will laugh at me. Still,
You say it would be a good
Idea. There's not much pleasure
In a sour stomach and
Bad breath. I really know that I
Ought to stop. If I don't do it,
I don't know what will happen to me.

MEI YAO CH'EN

48

OU YANG HSIU

LIV

WHEN THE MOON IS IN THE RIVER
OF HEAVEN

The frail branches of the arbor
Shelter the roses from the gusts of the East Wind.
Enveloped in a cloud of perfume
Filled with drops of dew.
For whom are they so seductive?
Is it only to provoke the fragile
Butterflies and the irascible bees?
My heart swollen with sentimentality,
I wander in this pleasure garden.
And then my drunkenness wears off,
My pleasure goes and does not return.
The moon, sad enough to tear the bowels,
Sinks to the horizon, and suddenly
The Spring has grown old.

OU YANG HSIU

XLIX

IN THE EVENING I WALK BY THE RIVER

The frozen river is drifted deep with snow.
For days, only a few spots near the bank have stayed open.
In the evening when everyone has gone home,
The cormorants roost on the boats of the fishermen.

OU YANG HSIU

L

FISHERMAN

The wind blows the line out from his fishing pole.
In a straw hat and grass cape the fisherman
Is invisible in the long reeds.
In the fine spring rain it is impossible to see very far
And the mist rising from the water has hidden the hills.

OU YANG HSIU

LI

SPRING WALK TO THE PAVILION OF GOOD CROPS AND PEACE

The trees are brilliant with flowers
And the hills are green.
The sun is about to set.
Over the immense plain
A green carpet of grass
Stretches to infinity.
The passersby do not care
That Spring is about to end.
Carelessly they come and go
Before the pavilion,
Trampling the fallen flowers.

OU YANG HSIU

LII

EAST WIND

The burgeoning trees are thick with leaves.
The birds are singing on all the hills.
The east wind blows softly.
The birds sing, the flowers dance.
This minor magistrate is drunk.
Tomorrow when he wakes up,
Spring will no longer be new.

OU YANG HSIU

LIII

GREEN JADE PLUM TREES IN SPRING

Spring comes early to the gardens
Of the South, with dancing flowers.
The gentle breeze carries the sound
Of horses whinnying. The blue
Green plums are already as large
As beans. The willow leaves are long,
And really are curved like a girl's
Eyebrows. Butterflies whirl in the
Long sunlight. In the evening the
Mist lies heavy on the flowers.
The grass is covered with dew.
Girls in their transparent dresses,
Indolent and lascivious,
Lounge in their hammocks. Swallows, two
By two, nest under the painted eaves.

OU YANG HSIU

XLIX

IN THE EVENING I WALK BY THE RIVER

The frozen river is drifted deep with snow.
For days, only a few spots near the bank have stayed open.
In the evening when everyone has gone home,
The cormorants roost on the boats of the fishermen.

OU YANG HSIU

L

FISHERMAN

The wind blows the line out from his fishing pole.
In a straw hat and grass cape the fisherman
Is invisible in the long reeds.
In the fine spring rain it is impossible to see very far
And the mist rising from the water has hidden the hills.

OU YANG HSIU

SPRING WALK TO THE PAVILION OF
GOOD CROPS AND PEACE

The trees are brilliant with flowers
And the hills are green.
The sun is about to set.
Over the immense plain
A green carpet of grass
Stretches to infinity.
The passersby do not care
That Spring is about to end.
Carelessly they come and go
Before the pavilion,
Trampling the fallen flowers.

OU YANG HSIU

LII

EAST WIND

The burgeoning trees are thick with leaves.
The birds are singing on all the hills.
The east wind blows softly.
The birds sing, the flowers dance.
This minor magistrate is drunk.
Tomorrow when he wakes up,
Spring will no longer be new.

OU YANG HSIU

GREEN JADE PLUM TREES IN SPRING

Spring comes early to the gardens
Of the South, with dancing flowers.
The gentle breeze carries the sound
Of horses whinnying. The blue
Green plums are already as large
As beans. The willow leaves are long,
And really are curved like a girl's
Eyebrows. Butterflies whirl in the
Long sunlight. In the evening the
Mist lies heavy on the flowers.
The grass is covered with dew.
Girls in their transparent dresses,
Indolent and lascivious,
Lounge in their hammocks. Swallows, two
By two, nest under the painted eaves.

OU YANG HSIU

WHEN THE MOON IS IN THE RIVER
OF HEAVEN

The frail branches of the arbor
Shelter the roses from the gusts of the East Wind.
Enveloped in a cloud of perfume
Filled with drops of dew.
For whom are they so seductive?
Is it only to provoke the fragile
Butterflies and the irascible bees?
My heart swollen with sentimentality,
I wander in this pleasure garden.
And then my drunkenness wears off,
My pleasure goes and does not return.
The moon, sad enough to tear the bowels,
Sinks to the horizon, and suddenly
The Spring has grown old.

OU YANG HSIU

SONG OF LIANG CHOU

Perfume blows from the kingfisher
Green trees. Bright as targets in
Their new dyed skirts, beautiful girls,
Hands joined, scamper amongst the
Odorous blossoms. Green shadows,
Red silhouettes. They lie on
Fine Persian rugs. They put flowers
In their hair to enhance their
Beauty. They look sidelong in
Their phoenix mirrors. I only
Fear that their painted faces
May vanish, and the spring evening
Will be unworthy of its
Name and spoiled of all charm.
In reality—
On the green moss, after the rain,
I have seen a few spots of
Scarlet. I opened my door
And went out for a stroll. Coming back,
I leaned long on the vermilion balcony.
The autumn fruits, hanging here
And there, are covered with the faint
Frost of ripeness. Their delicate
Veins of rose brought back those painted
Faces. Men, in moments of
Idleness, occupy their minds
With the vacuity of

Feminine eyebrows. Who ever
Has been benefitted by the
Presence of a woman? Still
My lewd heart yearns for the past.
Next year, once more, the Spring wind will
Start me thinking amorous thoughts.

OU YANG HSIU

LVI

READING THE POEMS OF AN ABSENT FRIEND

Tsu Mei is early dead. Chang Yu
Now is somewhere in the South.
And I, unhappy, am like
A four horse chariot which
Has lost the horses on right
And left. Their memory, like
A strong enemy, attacks
And overthrows me. The feeble
Swarm of my own thoughts struggles
In vain against the shock. All
Men respect hard work, but in
Leisure and repose they find
Happiness and peace. And me,
What is the matter with me?
Nothing, except that I cannot
Bear the loss of friends. It has
Been a long time since I have
Written a poem. My ideas
Are like sticky pudding. When
Good land is not cultivated
Regularly the grass vanishes
And is replaced by weeds, hard
To hoe. When you do not use
A well every day the pure
Water does not replace itself.
By chance, I opened a book
Of Mei's and I forgot

Everything else while the sun
Sank below the eaves. The joys
Of poetry, for those who
Appreciate them, increase with
Time and familiarity,
Their richness never ends in
Satiety. I am sorry
For the men of these times. They
Talk of nothing interesting
And have no ambition and
Die without ever being
Aware of the music of verse.
But I who am lucky enough
To appreciate these pleasures,
The more I savour, the deeper
I understand, the more I want.
In the leisure which my duties
Leave me, I stay at home, so
I can enjoy them undisturbed.
And I wonder that my feeble
Means have enabled me to
Enjoy these poems so much, that here
I have run off, like a horse
Whose rider has lost the bit.

OU YANG HSIU

AN ANSWER TO TING YUAN CH'EN

The Spring wind will never reach
Me on this distant frontier.
It is the second month, and
There are no flowers in the
Town or on the hills. Destructive
Snow breaks the branches where oranges
Should hang. Freezing wind and thunder
Drive the bamboo shoots back into
The earth. All night you can hear
The sad cries of the wild geese.
They make me think of my old home.
I have been sick since the new year.
The sight of flowers might cheer me
Up. I am no longer your guest,
Among the flowers at Lo Yang,
But even the wild flowers,
If they would only come would be
Enough to make me happier.

OU YANG HSIU

SPRING DAY ON WEST LAKE

The lovely Spring breeze has come
Back to the Lake of the West.
The Spring waters are so clear and
Green they might be freshly painted.
The clouds of perfume are sweeter
Than can be imagined. In the
Gentle East wind the petals
Fall like grains of rice. This old
Military counsellor,
Moved by the Spring, is filled with
Troubled thoughts. His white hairs, like
This poem, are a salute of
Autumn to Spring. He offers
The lake a cup of wine. He
Thinks of his comrades on the
Frontiers of Heaven, ten thousand
Miles away. The Spring moves the hearts
Of all men alike. Snow melts
From the passes. The mountains
Turn green. Flowers cover the
River banks. Under the full
Moon of April young men welcome
The Spring with wine and love. But
Me, once more greeting the Spring,
My head is white. I am in
A strange land, in the midst of
People whose ways are not mine.

The soft East wind is the only
Familiar thing from the old days.

OU YANG HSIU

LIX

OLD AGE

In the Springtime I am always
Sorry the nights are so short.
My lamp is burning out, the flame
Is low. Flying insects circle
About it. I am sick. My eyes
Are dry and dull. If I sit
Too long in one position,
All my bones ache. Chance thoughts from
I don't know where crowd upon me.
When I get to the end of a
Train of thought, I have forgotten
The beginning. For one thing
I retain I forget ten.
When I was young I liked to read.
Now I am too old to make
The effort. Then, too, if I come
Across something interesting
I have no one to talk to
About it. Sad and alone,
I sigh with self pity.

OU YANG HSIU

SU TUNG P'O

THE RED CLIFF

The River flows to the East.
Its waves have washed away all
The heroes of history.
To the West of the ancient
Wall you enter the Red Gorge
Of Chu Ko Liang of the
Days of the Three Kingdoms. The
Jagged peaks pierce the heavens.
The furious rapids beat
At the boat, and dash up in
A thousand clouds of spray like
Snow. Mountain and river have
Often been painted, in the
Memory of the heroes
Of those days. I remember
Long ago, Kung Ch'in newly
Married to the beautiful
Chiao-siao, shining in splendor,
A young warrior, and the other
Chu Ko Liang, in his blue cap,
Waving his horsetail duster,
Smiling and chatting as he
Burned the navy of Ts'ao Ts'ao.
Their ashes were scattered to
The four winds. They vanished away
In smoke. I like to dream of
Those dead kingdoms. Let people

Laugh at my prematurely
Grey hair. My answer is
A wine cup, full of the
Moon drowned in the River.

SU TUNG P'O

AT GOLD HILL MONASTERY

My native land is up there,
Far away, near the head of
The river. Just a wandering
Bureaucrat, I have been sent
To the spot where the river
Enters the sea. I have heard
That here, ten feet deep in the
Salt marsh, you can find traces
Of the sand, still cold, which bubbled
Up in the Chong Ling spring high
In the rocky plateau by
The Southern Trail. I have come
Here, following the currents
And waves. Now, high in the tower,
I overlook the whole countryside.
South of the river, north of
The river, the blue mountains
Are without number. The beauty
Of the evening cannot
Overcome my sorrow. I
Reenter my rowboat to
Return. The monks, in their lonely
Monastery, sit watching
The setting sun. The gentle breeze,
Over ten thousand acres,
Makes a fine brocade of the
Waters. In the last rays of

The twilight the schools of fish
Flicker in the water.
At this moment, out of the
River, the material
Soul of the moon is born.
Later, after the second
Watch, after the moon has set,
The heavens are left in profound
Blackness. Then in the heart of
The river, the basket torches
Of the fishermen gleam. Their
Lights come and go, shining against
The sky, and frightening the birds
Asleep on the water. I
Try to sleep, but my heart is
Troubled, my mind is distracted.
Neither men nor ghosts come here.
What is it then? Has the spirit
Of the river shown me a
Vision to warn me? Since the
River mouth and the islands
Affect me so, I will not come
Again to this monastery.
I thank the spirit of the river,
But what good has it done?
Just as its waters cannot
Return to their source, so I can
Never return to my native land.

SU TUNG P'O

ON THE DEATH OF HIS BABY SON

I will never be able to stop my tears.
And the day is far off when I will
Forget this cruel day.
Why could we not have died with him?
His little clothes still hang on his rack.
His milk is still by his bed.
Overcome, it is as though life had left us.
We lie prostrate and insensible all day.
I am no longer young enough
To try to understand what has happened.
I was warned of it in a dream.
No medicine would have helped,
Even if it had been heaped mountain high.
The disease took its course inexorably.
It would be better for me if I took
A sword and cut open my bowels.
They are already cut to pieces with sorrow.
I realize what I am doing
And try to come to myself again,
But I am exhausted and helpless,
Carried away by excess of sorrow.

SU TUNG P'O

THE TERRACE IN THE SNOW

In the golden twilight the rain
Was like silk threads. During the night
It cleared. The wind fell. It grew
Colder. My covers felt damp
And cold. Without my knowing it,
The snow had drifted into
The room like heaps of salt. At
The fifth watch, in the first flush
Of dawn, I close the curtain
Of the study. During the
Rest of the night I listen
To the ice, warping the colored
Tiles of the roof. In the morning
I sweep the Northern terrace
And look out at Saddle Peak.
It is clear of clouds and I
Can see both summits. Above
The village in the morning
Sunlight, crows begin to circle.
The mud of the streets is covered
With white. No cart track has marked it.
Ice has turned the shop roofs to
White jade. Snow has filled the doorways
With rice. The last cicadas
Have long since gone to earth. Now
They will have to dig a thousand
Feet deeper. Some clouds pile up,

The color of dried moss. My
Chest bothers me again.
I feel I have lost the
Ability to write.
The icicles on the eaves
Drone in the wind like the swords
Of murderers.

SU TUNG P'O

LXIV

THE WEAKER THE WINE

*"The weakest wine is better than warm water.
Rags are better than no clothes at all.
An ugly wife and a quarrelsome concubine
Are better than an empty house."*

The weaker the wine,
The easier it is to drink two cups.
The thinner the robe,
The easier it is to wear it double.
Ugliness and beauty are opposites,
But when you're drunk, one is as good as the other.
Ugly wives and quarrelsome concubines,
The older they grow, the more they're alike.
Live unknown if you would realize your end.
Follow the advice of your common sense.
Avoid the Imperial Audience
Chamber, the Eastern Flowery Hall.
The dust of the times and the wind of the Northern Pass.
One hundred years is a long time,
But at last it comes to an end.
Meanwhile it is no greater accomplishment
To be a rich corpse or a poor one.
Jewels of jade and pearl are put in the mouths
Of the illustrious dead
To conserve their bodies.
They do them no good, but after a thousand years,
They feed the robbers of their tombs.
As for literature, it is its own reward.

72

Fortunately fools pay little attention to it.
A chance for graft
Makes them blush with joy.
Good men are their own worst enemies.
Wine is the best reward of merit.
In all the world, good and evil,
Joy and sorrow, are in fact
Only aspects of the Void.

SU TUNG P'O

THE LAST DAY OF THE YEAR

The year about to end
Is like a snake creeping in a field.
You have no sooner seen it
Than it has half disappeared.
It is gone and its trouble is gone with it.
It would be worse if you could catch it by its tail.
Why bother to try when it will do you no good?
The children are awake, they can't sleep.
They sit up all night laughing and chattering.
The cocks do not cry to announce the dawn.
The watch do not beat on their drums.
Everybody stays up while the lamps burn low,
And goes out to watch the stars fade and set.
I hope next year will be better than last.
But I know it will be just the
Same old mistakes and mischances.
Maybe I will have accomplished
More next New Year's Eve.
I should. I am still young and full of confidence.

SU TUNG P'O

LXVI

HARVEST SACRIFICE

The crops are all gathered.
The work of the year draws to an end.
If you have no bronze vessels for sacrifice
You can always borrow them. Others have plenty.
Mountains and rivers have given up their produce,
In varying quantities to the poor and the rich.
Some offer plates of fat carp.
Some offer baskets with pairs of rabbits.
The rich prepare banquets.
Silk and bright brocade decorate their halls.
The poor have hardly anything to offer.
Instead, they try to hide
The family mortar from the tax assessor.
I am a stranger in this neighborhood,
Where gay processions fill the streets and alleys.
I too sing the old folksongs,
But I sing to myself, no one sings with me.

SU TUNG P'O

LXVII

A WALK IN THE COUNTRY

The spring wind raises fine dust from the road.
Everybody is out, enjoying the new leaves.
Strollers are drinking in the inns along the way.
Cart wheels roll over the young grass.
The whole town has gone to the suburbs.
Children scamper everywhere and shout to the skies.
Songs and drum beats scare the hills
And make the leaves tremble on the trees.
Picnic baskets and jugs litter the fields
And put the crows and kites to flight.
Who is that fellow who has gathered a crowd?
He says he is a Taoist monk.
He is selling charms to the passersby.
He shouts, waves his hands, rolls his eyes.
"If you raise silk, these will
Grow cocoons as big as pitchers.
If you raise stock, these will
Make the sheep as big as elks."
Nobody really believes him.
It is the spirit of spring in him they are buying.
As soon as he has enough money
He will go fill himself with wine
And fall down drunk,
Overcome by the magic of his own charms.

SU TUNG P'O

TO A TRAVELER

Last year when I accompanied you
As far as the Yang Chou Gate,
The snow was flying, like white willow cotton.
This year, Spring has come again,
And the willow cotton is like snow.
But you have not come back.
Alone before the open window,
I raise my wine cup to the shining moon.
The wind, moist with evening dew,
Blows the gauze curtains.
Maybe Chang-O the moon goddess,
Will pity this single swallow
And join us together with the cord of light
That reaches beneath the painted eaves of your home.

SU TUNG P'O

LXIX

THE PURPLE PEACH TREE

Timidly, still half asleep, it has blossomed.
Afraid of the teeth of the frost, it was late this year.
Now its crimson mixes with the
Brilliance of the cherries and apricots.
Unique, it is more beautiful than snow and hoar frost.
Under the cold, its heart awoke to the Spring season.
Full of wine, sprawling on the alabaster table,
I dream of the ancient poet who could not distinguish
The peach, the cherry and the apricot, except by their
Green leaves and dark branches.

SU TUNG P'O

LXX

THE SHADOW OF FLOWERS

It piles up, thick and formidable, on the marble terrace.
The pages, called again and again, try to sweep it away.
Just then, the sun comes out and carries it off.
But never mind, the next moon
The shadow will come back.

SU TUNG P'O

THE END OF THE YEAR

When a friend starts on a journey of a thousand miles,
As he is about to leave, he delays again and again.
When men part, they feel they may never meet again.
When a year has gone, how will you ever find it again?
I wonder where it has gone, this year that is ended?
Certainly someplace far beyond the horizon.
It is gone like a river which flows to the East,
And empties into the sea without hope of return.
My neighbors on the left are heating wine.
On the right they are roasting a fat pig.
They will have one day of joy
As recompense for a whole year of trouble.
We leave the bygone year without regret.
Will we leave so carelessly the years to come?
Everything passes, everything
Goes, and never looks back,
And we grow older and less strong.

SU TUNG P'O

LXXII

ON THE SIU CHENG ROAD

A gentle East wind is blowing.
I travel through the mountains.
White clouds rest on the peaks like
Caps of silk floss. Over
The tree tops the sun gleams like
A polished cymbal. Peach trees
Bloom beyond bamboo fences.
Along the streams, willows wave
Above the pools. The mountaineers
Of the West know how to be
Happy, full of melon soup
And fried bamboo shoots after
The spring sowing.

SU TUNG P'O

LXXIII

THOUGHTS IN EXILE

I lift my head and watch
The phoenix and the snowy swan
Cross the heavens in their migrations.
Wealth, office, position,
After all these years, mean nothing to me.
The foundered horse no longer
Hopes to travel a thousand miles.
In exile, in autumn,
I grow lazy and indifferent.
In history men have
Always been treated like this.
I am forbidden to visit the Western Lake.
There is no place else I want to go.
The wise man, no matter how he is treated,
Knows that Heaven does nothing without reason.
But nobody can stop me
From writing poems about the
Mountains and rivers of Wu.

SU TUNG P'O

LOOKING FROM THE PAVILION OVER
THE LAKE
27TH, 6TH MONTH. WRITTEN WHILE DRUNK

Black clouds spread over the sky
Like ink. I can no longer
See the mountains. Hailstones rebound
From the roofs of the boats.
A whirlwind sweeps out from the
Shore and is suddenly gone.
From the pavilion over
The lake the water has become
Indistinguishable from the sky.

SU TUNG P'O

THE SOUTHERN ROOM OVER THE RIVER

The room is prepared, the incense burned.
I close the shutters before I close my eyelids.
The patterns of the quilt repeat the waves of the river.
The gauze curtain is like a mist.
Then a dream comes to me and when I awake
I no longer know where I am.
I open the western window and watch the waves
Stretching on and on to the horizon.

SU TUNG P'O

LXXVI

EPIGRAM

I fish for minnows in the lake.
Just born, they have no fear of man.
And those who have learned,
Never come back to warn them.

SU TUNG P'O

LXXVII

AT THE WASHING OF MY SON

Everybody wants an intelligent son.
My intelligence only got me into difficulties.
I want only a brave and simple boy,
Who, without trouble or resistance,
Will rise to the highest offices.

SU TUNG P'O

LXXVIII

MOON, FLOWERS, MAN

I raise my cup and invite
The moon to come down from the
Sky. I hope she will accept
Me. I raise my cup and ask
The branches, heavy with flowers,
To drink with me. I wish them
Long life and promise never
To pick them. In company
With the moon and the flowers,
I get drunk, and none of us
Ever worries about good
Or bad. How many people
Can comprehend our joy? I
Have wine and moon and flowers.
Who else do I want for drinking companions?

SU TUNG P'O

85

LXXIX

BEGONIAS

The East wind blows gently.
The rising rays float
On the thick perfumed mist.
The moon appears, right there,
At the corner of the balcony.
I only fear in the depth of night
The flowers will fall asleep.
I hold up a gilded candle
To shine on their scarlet beauty.

SU TUNG P'O

LXXX

RAIN IN THE ASPENS

My neighbor to the East has
A grove of aspens. Tonight
The rain sounds mournfully in
Them. Alone, at my window,
I cannot sleep. Autumn insects
Swarm, attracted by my light.

SU TUNG P'O

LXXXI

THE TURNING YEAR

Nightfall. Clouds scatter and vanish.
The sky is pure and cold.
Silently the River of Heaven turns in the Jade Vault.
If tonight I do not enjoy life to the full,
Next month, next year, who knows where I will be?

SU TUNG P'O

LXXXII

AUTUMN

The water lilies of summer are gone. They are no more.
Nothing remains but their umbrella leaves.
The chrysanthemums of Autumn are fading.
Their leaves are white with frost.
The beauty of the year is only a solemn memory.
Soon it will be winter and
Oranges turn gold and the citrons green.

SU TUNG P'O

LXXXIII

SPRING NIGHT

The few minutes of a Spring night
Are worth ten thousand pieces of gold.
The perfume of the flowers is so pure.
The shadows of the moon are so black.
In the pavilion the voices and flutes are so high and light.
In the garden a hammock rocks
In the night so deep, so profound.

SU TUNG P'O

SPRING

The pear blossoms are pure
White against the blue green willows.
The willow cotton blows in the wind.
The city is full of flying pear flowers.
The petals fallen on the balcony look like snow.
How many Spring Festivals are we born to see?

SU TUNG P'O

LI CH'ING CHAO

AUTUMN EVENING BESIDE THE LAKE

Wind passes over the lake.
The swelling waves stretch away
Without limit. Autumn comes with the twilight,
And boats grow rare on the river.
Flickering waters and fading mountains
Always touch the heart of man.
I never grow tired of singing
Of their boundless beauty.
The lotus pods are already formed,
And the water lilies have grown old.
The dew has brightened the blossoms
Of the arrowroot along the riverbank.
The herons and seagulls sleep
On the sand with their
Heads tucked away, as though
They did not wish to see
The men who pass by on the river.

THE POETESS LI CH'ING CHAO

LXXXVI

TWO SPRINGS

Spring has come to the Pass.
Once more the new grass is kingfisher green.
The pink buds of the peach trees
Are still unopened little balls.
The clouds are milk white jade
Bordered and spotted with green jade.
No dust stirs.
In a dream that was too easy to read,
I have already drained and broken
The cup of Spring.
Flower shadows lie heavy
On the translucent curtains.
The full, transparent moon
Rises in the orange twilight.
Three times in two years
My lord has gone away to the East.
Today he returns.
And my joy is already
Greater than the Spring.

LI CH'ING CHAO

LXXXVII

QUAIL SKY

The icy sun rises silently
Across the closed window.
The Autumn leaves are falling fast
After last night's black frost.
A little wine makes the return
To tea more enjoyable.
I lay aside my bitter revery,
And enjoy the perfume that rises to my head.
Autumn ends, the nights grow long.
If I indulged my sad heart
The days would be still more
Frozen and sad. It is better
To encourage my frivolity,
And get drunk with the aroma
Of my wine cup.
I refuse to be burdened
By the yellowing heart
Of the chrysanthemum
Along the wall.

LI CH'ING CHAO

ALONE IN THE NIGHT

The warm rain and pure wind
Have just freed the willows from
The ice. As I watch the peach trees,
Spring rises from my heart and blooms on
My cheeks. My mind is unsteady,
As if I were drunk. I try
To write a poem in which
My tears will flow together
With your tears. My rouge is stale.
My hairpins are too heavy.
I throw myself across my
Gold cushions, wrapped in my lonely
Doubled quilt, and crush the phoenixes
In my headdress. Alone, deep
In bitter loneliness, without
Even a good dream, I lie,
Trimming the lamp in the passing night.

LI CH'ING CHAO

LXXXIX

TO THE TUNE,
"PLUM BLOSSOMS FALL AND SCATTER"

The perfume of the red water lilies
Dies away. The Autumn air
Penetrates the pearl jade curtain.
Torches gleam on the orchid boats.
Who has sent me a message
Of love from the clouds? It is
The time when the wild swans
Return. The moonlight floods the women's
Quarters. Flowers, after their
Nature, whirl away in the wind.
Spilt water, after its nature,
Flows together at the lowest point.
Those who are of one being
Can never stop thinking of each other.
But, ah, my dear, we are apart,
And I have become used to sorrow.
This love—nothing can ever
Make it fade or disappear.
For a moment it was on my eyebrows,
Now it is heavy in my heart.

LI CH'ING CHAO

THE DAY OF COLD FOOD

Clear and bright is the splendor
Of Spring on the Day of Cold Food.
The dying smoke rises from
The jade animal like a
Silk thread floating in water.
I dream on a pile of cushions,
Amongst scattered and broken hair ornaments.
The swallows have not come back
From the Southern Sea, but already
Men begin again, fighting for straws.
Petals fly from the peach trees
Along the river. Willow catkins
Fill the air with floss. And then—
In the orange twilight—fall
Widely spaced drops of rain.

LI CH'ING CHAO

MIST

In my narrow room, I throw
Wide the window, and let in
The profound lasciviousness
Of Spring. Confused shadows
Flicker on the half drawn curtains.
Hidden in the pavilion, wordlessly,
I strum the rose jade harp.
Far away a rocky cliff
Falls from the mountain in the
Early twilight. A gentle breeze
Blows the mist like a shadow
Across my curtain. O bright pods
Of the pepper plant, you do not
Need to bow and beg pardon.
I know you cannot hold back
The passing day.

LI CH'ING CHAO

LXXXIX

TO THE TUNE,
"PLUM BLOSSOMS FALL AND SCATTER"

The perfume of the red water lilies
Dies away. The Autumn air
Penetrates the pearl jade curtain.
Torches gleam on the orchid boats.
Who has sent me a message
Of love from the clouds? It is
The time when the wild swans
Return. The moonlight floods the women's
Quarters. Flowers, after their
Nature, whirl away in the wind.
Spilt water, after its nature,
Flows together at the lowest point.
Those who are of one being
Can never stop thinking of each other.
But, ah, my dear, we are apart,
And I have become used to sorrow.
This love—nothing can ever
Make it fade or disappear.
For a moment it was on my eyebrows,
Now it is heavy in my heart.

LI CH'ING CHAO

XC

THE DAY OF COLD FOOD

Clear and bright is the splendor
Of Spring on the Day of Cold Food.
The dying smoke rises from
The jade animal like a
Silk thread floating in water.
I dream on a pile of cushions,
Amongst scattered and broken hair ornaments.
The swallows have not come back
From the Southern Sea, but already
Men begin again, fighting for straws.
Petals fly from the peach trees
Along the river. Willow catkins
Fill the air with floss. And then—
In the orange twilight—fall
Widely spaced drops of rain.

LI CH'ING CHAO

MIST

In my narrow room, I throw
Wide the window, and let in
The profound lasciviousness
Of Spring. Confused shadows
Flicker on the half drawn curtains.
Hidden in the pavilion, wordlessly,
I strum the rose jade harp.
Far away a rocky cliff
Falls from the mountain in the
Early twilight. A gentle breeze
Blows the mist like a shadow
Across my curtain. O bright pods
Of the pepper plant, you do not
Need to bow and beg pardon.
I know you cannot hold back
The passing day.

LI CH'ING CHAO

陸

游

THE WILD FLOWER MAN

Do you know the old man who
Sells flowers by the South Gate?
He lives on flowers like a bee.
In the morning he sells mallows,
In the evening he has poppies.
His shanty roof lets in the
Blue sky. His rice bin is
Always empty. When he has
Made enough money from his
Flowers, he heads for a teahouse.
When his money is gone, he
Gathers some more flowers.
All the spring weather, while the
Flowers are in bloom, he is
In bloom, too. Every day he
Is drunk all day long. What does
He care if new laws are posted
At the Emperor's palace?
What does it matter to him
If the government is built
On sand? If you try to talk
To him, he won't answer but
Only give you a drunken
Smile from under his tousled hair.

LU YU

XCIII

PHOENIX HAIRPINS

Pink and white hands like roses and rice cake!
Cups full of golden pools of wine!
Today the willows are blooming
By the palace wall. The Spring wind
Brings me no pleasure and I
Hate it. My bowels are knotted
With bitterness. I cannot
Loosen the cord of the years
Which has bound us together.
The Spring is still the Spring
Of other days, but I am
Empty, withered with pain.
My rouge is streaked with tears, my
Dress is stained with tear drops.
The peach trees are in blossom
Over my room, here by the
Still lake that mirrors the hills.
I no longer have the strength
To finish this letter and
Wrap it in cloth of gold. When
You receive it, everything
Will be over forever.

LU YU

LEAVING THE MONASTERY EARLY
IN THE MORNING

In bed, asleep, I dream
I am a butterfly.
A crowing cock wakes me
Like a blow. The sun rises
Between foggy mountains.
Mist hides the distant crags.
My long retreat is over.
My worries begin again.
Laughing monks are gathering
Branches of peach blossoms
For a farewell present.
But no stirrup cup will sustain
Me on my journey back
Into a world of troubles.

LU YU

XCV

RAIN ON THE RIVER

In the fog we drift hither
And yon over the dark waves.
At last our little boat finds
Shelter under a willow bank.
At midnight I am awake,
Heavy with wine. The smoky
Lamp is still burning. The rain
Is still sighing in the bamboo
Thatch of the cabin of the boat.

LU YU

EVENING IN THE VILLAGE

Here in the mountain village
Evening falls peacefully.
Half tipsy, I lounge in the
Doorway. The moon shines in the
Twilit sky. The breeze is so
Gentle the water is hardly
Ruffled. I have escaped from
Lies and trouble. I no longer
Have any importance. I
Do not miss my horses and
Chariots. Here at home I
Have plenty of pigs and chickens.

LU YU

XCVII

I WALK OUT INTO THE COUNTRY AT NIGHT

The moon is so high it is
Almost in the Great Bear.
I walk out of the city
Along the road to the West.
The damp wind ruffles my coat.
Dewy grass soaks my sandals.
Fishermen are singing
On the distant river.
Fox fires dance on the ruined tombs.
A chill wind rises and fills
Me with melancholy. I
Try to think of words that will
Capture the uncanny solitude.
I come home late. The night
Is half spent. I stand for a
Long while in the doorway.
My young son is still up, reading.
Suddenly he bursts out laughing,
And all the sadness of the
Twilight of my life is gone.

LU YU

XCVIII

IDLENESS

I keep the rustic gate closed
For fear somebody might step
On the green moss. The sun grows
Warmer. You can tell it's Spring.
Once in a while, when the breeze
Shifts, I can hear the sounds of the
Village. My wife is reading
The classics. Now and then she
Asks me the meaning of a word.
I call for wine and my son
Fills my cup till it runs over.
I have only a little
Garden, but it is planted
With yellow and purple plums.

LU YU

NIGHT THOUGHTS

I cannot sleep. The long, long
Night is full of bitterness.
I sit alone in my room,
Beside a smoky lamp.
I rub my heavy eyelids
And idly turn the pages
Of my book. Again and again
I trim my brush and stir the ink.
The hours go by. The moon comes
In the open window, pale
And bright like new money.
At last I fall asleep and
I dream of the days on the
River at Tsa-feng, and the
Friends of my youth in Yen Chao.
Young and happy we ran
Over the beautiful hills.
And now the years have gone by,
And I have never gone back.

LU YU

C

I GET UP AT DAWN

When your teeth decay you cannot
Grow new ones. When your hair falls
Out you cannot plant it again.
I get up at dawn and look
At myself in the mirror.
My face is wrinkled, my hair
Is grey. I am filled with pity
For the years that are gone like
Spilt water. It can't be helped.
I take a cup of wine and
Turn to the bookcase once more.
Back through the centuries I
Visit Shun and Yu the Great
And Kue Lung, that famous rowdy.
Across three thousand years I
Can still see them plainly.
What does it matter? My flesh,
Like theirs, wears away with time.

LU YU

AUTUMN THOUGHTS

Great fame can be obtained
By routing an army
With oxen carrying
Burning straw on their horns.
But after all, it is
No more important than
The tracks of sandpipers
On a wave washed beach.
Days go by and become
A year and I am too
Lazy to notice. The
Business of Heaven
Vanishes in a wine cup.
By the river they are
Beating cloth for winter.
Moonlight penetrates the
Forest. The trees are losing
Their leaves. Autumn has come
To my withered garden.
I decide to climb to some
High place to enjoy the view.
But I can only manage
The hundred steps of the
Yuan Hung pagoda.

LU YU

SAILING ON THE LAKE TO THE CHING RIVER

It is Spring on the lake and
I run six or seven miles.
Sunset, I notice a few
Houses. Children are driving
Home the ducks and geese. Young girls
Are coming home carrying
Mulberry leaves and hemp. Here
In this hidden village the
Old ways still go on. The crops
Are good. Everybody is
Laughing. This old man fastens
His boat and climbs up the bank.
Tipsy, he holds fast to the vines.

LU YU

CHU HSI

朱熹

THE BOATS ARE AFLOAT

Last night along the river banks
The floods of Spring have risen.
Great warships and huge barges
Float as lightly as feathers.
Before, nothing could move them from the mud.
Today they swim with ease in the swift current.

CHU HSI

CIV

SPRING SUN

On the Day of Cold Food
I go out to smell the perfume of the flowers,
Along the bank of the river.
Happy and at ease,
I let the soft East wind bathe my face.
Everywhere the Spring is blazing
With ten thousand shades of blue
And ten thousand colors of red.

CHU HSI

THE FARM BY THE LAKE

For ten miles the mountains rise
Above the lake. The beauty
Of water and mountain is
Impossible to describe.
In the glow of evening
A traveller sits in front
Of an inn, sipping wine.
The moon shines above a
Little bridge and a single
Fisherman. Around the farm
A bamboo fence descends to
The water. I chat with an
Old man about work and crops.
Maybe, when the years have come
When I can lay aside my
Cap and robe of office,
I can take a little boat
And come back to this place.

CHU HSI

THOUGHTS WHILE READING

The mirror of the pond gleams,
Half an acre in size.
The splendor of the sky,
And the whiteness of the clouds
Are reflected back upon themselves.
I ask the pond where I can find
Anything else as pure and transparent.
"Only in the springs of the water of life."

CHU HSI

HSU CHAO

THE LOCUST SWARM

Locusts laid their eggs in the corpse
Of a soldier. When the worms were
Mature, they took wing. Their drone
Was ominous, their shells hard.
Anyone could tell they had hatched
From an unsatisfied anger.
They flew swiftly towards the North.
They hid the sky like a curtain.
When the wife of the soldier
Saw them, she turned pale, her breath
Failed her. She knew he was dead
In battle, his corpse lost in
The desert. That night she dreamed
She rode a white horse, so swift
It left no footprints, and came
To where he lay in the sand.
She looked at his face, eaten
By the locusts, and tears of
Blood filled her eyes. Ever after
She would not let her children
Injure any insect which
Might have fed on the dead. She
Would lift her face to the sky
And say, "O locusts, if you
Are seeking a place to winter,
You can find shelter in my heart."

HSU CHAO

CHU SHU CHEN

朱淑真

CVIII

PLAINT

Spring flowers, Autumn moons,
Water lilies still carry
Away my heart like a lost
Boat. As long as I am flesh
And bone I will never find
Rest. There will never come a
Time when I will be able
To resist my emotions.

CHU SHU CHEN

CIX

HYSTERIA

When I look in the mirror
My face frightens me. I am
Afraid of myself. Every
Spring weakness overcomes me like
A mortal sickness. I am too
Weary to arrange the flowers
Or paint my face. Everything
Bothers me. All the old sorrows
Flood back and make the present worse.
The crying nightjars terrify me.
The mating swallows embarrass me,
Flying two by two outside
My window. Plucked eyebrows,
Weary eyes—that have grown hard
With loneliness. Swallows chirp
In the painted eaves—but I
Have lost the ability
Even to dream of happiness.
Each new Spring finds me deeper
Tangled and snarled in bitterness.
As all the world grows more lovely
My bowels are torn with sorrow.
Peach blossoms quiver in the
Light of the new moon on the first
Nights of the Season of Cold Food.
Huge willows in the golden
Twilight wave their long shadows

In the clear bright winds of Spring.
Surrounded by flowers, trapped in
Pain, I watch the sun set beyond
The roofs of the women's quarters.

CHU SHU CHEN

CX

SPRING

Spring has come. I try to forget
All the old quarrels and anguish.
In the gentle breeze, in the clear
Brightness all things should start anew.
But why do the birds all hate me?
And why do the flowers betray me?
And why do the peach and cherry
Blossoms prostrate me? Tears streak
The paint on my cheeks. My girdle
Is too loose for my starved body.
When spring comes with the third moon,
I know I am a burden
To my lord. But, O my lord,
In the third moon of spring the East
Wind is a heavy burden to me.

CHU SHU CHEN

THE OLD ANGUISH

Sheltered from the Spring wind by
A silver screen, I doze in my
Folded quilt, cold and alone.
I start awake at the cry
Of a bird—my dream is gone.
The same sorrow, the same headache
Return. Thick shadows of flowers
Darken the filigree lattice.
Incense coils over the screen
And spirals past my pillow.
The oriole is not to blame
For a broken dream of a
Bygone Spring. I sit with my
Old anguish as the evening fades.

CHU SHU CHEN

MORNING

I get up. I am sick of
Rouging my cheeks. My face in
The mirror disgusts me. My
Thin shoulders are bowed with
Hopelessness. Tears of loneliness
Well up in my eyes. Wearily
I open my toilet table.
I arch and paint my eyebrows
And steam my heavy braids.
My maid is so stupid that she
Offers me plum blossoms for my hair.

CHU SHU CHEN

CXIII

STORMY NIGHT IN AUTUMN

Like a flight of arrows the wind
Pierces my curtain. The cold rain
Roars like the drum of the nightwatch.
My breasts are freezing. Huddled
In my folded quilt, I cannot sleep.
My bowels and liver are like lead.
My tears flow without stopping.
The bamboos outside my window
Sob like the broken heart of Autumn.
Rain beats on the painted tiles.
This night will never end. Freezing,
Alone in the dark, I am
Going mad, counting my sorrows.
My heart pounds as if it would break.
Inside my body, thin as a
Stem of bamboo, my bowels
Twist and knot. How will I ever
Escape from this torture? Outside
My window now I hear the rain
Rattle on the banana trees.
Each beaten leaf contains
Ten thousand pains.

CHU SHU CHEN

ALONE

I raise the curtains and go out
To watch the moon. Leaning on the
Balcony, I breathe the evening
Wind from the west, heavy with the
Odors of decaying Autumn.
The rose jade of the river
Blends with the green jade of the void.
Hidden in the grass a cricket chirps.
Hidden in the sky storks cry out.
I turn over and over in
My heart the memories of
Other days. Tonight as always
There is no one to share my thoughts.

CHU SHU CHEN

Tu Fu (713-770) is, in my opinion, and in the opinion of a majority of those qualified to speak, the greatest non-epic, non dramatic poet who has survived in any language. Sappho, for instance, can hardly be said to have survived. He shares with her, Catullus, and Baudelaire, his only possible competitors, a sensibility acute past belief. Like them, he is— possibly paying the price of such a sensibility—considerable of a neurasthenic and the creator of an elaborate poetic personality, a fictional character half mask, half revelation. Tu Fu came from a family of scholars, officials, and landowners, and rose early to a minor office in the court of Hsuan Tsung, called Ming Huang, the Bright Emperor. With the majority of the scholar class, he was opposed violently to the party of Yang Kuei Fei, the Emperor's famous concubine. Following the legendary histories of the first dynasties, the disasters that smote the Chinese throne were traditionally attributed to the evils of women, eunuchs, wine, and magic, and Ming Huang was no exception.

Actually, Yang Kuei Fei, her family and lovers were the inner core of an imperialist party in the Chinese court. Outlanders and upstarts of various sorts, themselves products of a kind of internationalism, they realized that T'ang China could only survive at its then great extent by admitting the associated peoples of the inner Asian frontiers to a share of power and a measure of federated autonomy. This of course was rank atheist nihilism to the Confucian literati. The court struggle led eventually to the overthrow of Yang Kuo Chung, Yang Kuei Fei's brother; the revolt of An Lu Shan, her Turkish lover; the flight of the court; the execution, during the flight, at the insistence of the orthodox party, of Yang Kuei Fei; the abdication of the Emperor; the recapture of the capital by the troops of his son; and finally the fall of the capital again to the Nan Chao federation of Yunnanese and Tibetans. For a generation the most stable area in China was the isolated Southwest province of Szechuan—a situation not unlike the recent period of Japanese invasion and civil wars. The T'ang Dynasty was crippled permanently. The greatest period of

Chinese civilization in the Christian era entered a slow decline from which it never recovered and the seeds were sown of a parochial chauvinism which kept the so-called geo-political problems of China unsolved until now.

Although Tu Fu's young days were spent at Ming Huang's spectacularly brilliant court, familiar to most Western readers from the work of Li Po, his maturity was passed in a time of trouble, wandering, exile, chronic insecurity. He became a Court Censor, a kind of Tribune of the Patricians, under Su Tsung, Ming Huang's son. This job was in reality an empty sinecure. Tu Fu, an unregenerate believer in the classics, proceeded to admonish the Emperor on his morals and foreign policy and was summarily dismissed. The longest settled period in his life follôwed, in a "thatched hut" in the suburbs of Ch'eng-tu in Szechuan. It may have had a grass roof but it was doubtless quite palatial by any other standards than those of the imperial palace. He was happy, as men usually are, in quiet revery over vanished glories and a ruined career. Political changes started him wandering again slowly down the river, always hoping to return to the capital. His last years were spent largely in a houseboat. At 59 he died, apparently still in his boat. Various legends grew up about his death. Possibly he died of exposure due to the vicissitudes of storm and flood on the river.

All through his life Tu Fu wrote fulldress poems of advice to the throne. Most of these are the expected thing, full of wisdom as a Papal Christmas message, but in time he seems to have learned. Almost alone of his class, at the end of his days he came to hope for a united Chinese commonwealth, under a somewhat less pretentious, or, like the British, more etherialized, cult of the throne. I have not translated any of these poems. Others have done them well. They would require too much explanation. However well-intentioned, they savor of the social lie, at least to my taste, and do not interest me. I have chosen only those poems whose appeal is simple and direct, with a minimum of allusion to past literature or contemporary politics, in other words, poems that speak to me of situations in life like my own. I have thought of my translations as, finally, expressions of myself.

I do not wish to give the impression that Tu Fu is faultless.

He was a member of the scholar gentry and suffered from their ethnocentrism and caste consciousness, however transfigured. He was a valetudinarian. By the time he was thirty he was referring to himself as an aged white-haired man. He constantly speaks of his home as a hut and complains of his poverty, while in other poems, written at the same time, he reveals that he was moderately rich. He seems never to have relinquished ownership of his various farms, "grass huts," and probably always drew revenue or at least credit from them. It is greatly to be doubted if either he or any of his family ever suffered from hunger, let alone starvation. True, he says his son starved to death, but this may be only a literary extension. With the collapse of central authority and the resultant famine many people died of starvation. His son died at the same time, more likely from pestilence. He seems to have had only a mild literary affection for his wife. He wrote no love poems to women. Like most of his caste then and now his passionate relationships were with men. But these are not even minor faults—they are conventions, literary, caste, or Chinese. They are certainly microscopic spots compared with the blemishes that envelop Baudelaire like blankets. Behind the conventions is a humanity as deep and wise as Homer's.

Tu Fu comes from a saner, older, more secular culture than Homer and it is not a new discovery with him that the gods, the abstractions and forces of nature, are frivolous, lewd, vicious, quarrelsome, and cruel, and only men's steadfastness, love, magnanimity, calm, and compassion redeem the nightbound world. It is not a discovery, culturally or historically, but it is the essence of his being as a poet. If Isaiah is the greatest religious poet, Tu Fu is not religious at all. But for me his response to the human situation is the only kind of religion likely to outlast this century. "Reverence for life," it has been called. I have saturated myself with his poetry for thirty years. I am sure he has made me a better man, as a moral agent and as a perceiving organism. I say this because I feel that, above a certain level of attainment, the greatest poetry answers out of hand the problems of the critic and the esthetician. Poetry like Tu Fu's is the answer to the question, "What is the purpose of Art?"

137

I. "Checkered" is in deference to Mrs. Ayscough's reading of "hsien," which, with some justice, annoys Mr. Hung. I feel it does give an added concreteness. This poem is usually put with those of Tu Fu's youthful wanderyears, but it may be late.

II. "Younger brother" is a term of intimacy and does not mean necessarily an actual brother, though it is applied commonly to persons of the same surname. Lines 3 and 4 refer in Chinese to the red and green decorations for the New Year table, especially the pepper plant.

VI. The Chinese see a toad, a rabbit and mortar, a tree, and a girl, Chang-O, in the moon, where we see a face. This festival of the Harvest Moon is still celebrated by American Chinese with mooncakes of nuts, fruit, or bean paste, and with girls dancing like Chang-O.

VII. Almost every line in this poem has more than one possible translation. My version stays fairly close to the commentators, though it would have been interesting to see how far away from them I could get.

IX. This is a political poem. Tu Fu objects to the clandestine comings and goings. It is a standard set piece in Far Eastern poetry. The Japanese were able to boil it down to a haiku—"Jewels tinkle. The cold night drags." Audiences began at dawn in the Chinese and Japanese courts until the twentieth century.

X. Rhinoceros-horn cups didn't hold much liquor. The characters for the stars have had different meanings at different times. I believe they refer to Antares and a winter star.

XI. The throne distributed clothing and silk to the courtiers and bureaucrats as annual, usually New Year, gifts, as in the *Tale of Genji*. This custom survived in Japan and Annam until recently. Again, this is a set piece, in imitation of T'ao Ch'ien. Tu Fu seems in fact to have been a frugal drinker.

XIII. Tu Fu means that the poems, as the best possible descendants, will always perform the ancestral rites—the sentiment of Horace and Shakespeare. When no one remained to honor a dead man's tablet, his ghost, to all intents, ceased to exist. This translation was originally a Christmas present to my friend, Richard Eberhart.

XV. I have usually disguised these strict antitheses slightly by lineation or syntax, but not, for an example, here.

XIX. This is the famous "thatched hut" near Ch'eng-tu. It was probably far from being a hut, even if it was thatched. Tu Fu consistently poses as very poor, a literary convention. Internal evidence of the poems indicates that he was quite rich. T'ang China bequeathed to Japan, where it still survives, a pleasant taste for sophisticated rusticity.

XXVII. Eastern Wu, the lake region of what was then Southern China, seemed, and still seems, a paradisal region to the Chinese. Soochow and Hangchow are the oldest and greatest pleasure cities in the world.

XXXI. This is quite a free translation, rather simplified.

XXXII. "Tiger's Trail" may be the proper name of a highway, like other such terms in Tu Fu, for instance, "Rhinoceros Track" on Szechuan. The lines about the lamps and the watchman are obscurely phrased. Nobody is sure exactly what they mean.

XXXIV. The last two poems are not in chronological order, but they seem to me to give a perfect picture of Tu Fu's last days. "Brimming Water" was Mrs. Ayscough's inspired rendering of the title, and can't be bettered.

MEI YAO CH'EN (1002-1060) was an important courtier, official, and poet of the Sung Dynasty. His discursive style with its new subjectivity carried to their conclusion in a new kind of poetry the tendencies which began to manifest themselves at the end of T'ang. With Ou Yang Hsiu he is one of the founders of the Sung style. The West knows the landscape paintings of the time, full of revery over the essence of being. I have always felt a decided resemblance to Western poetry in his work. Ou Yang Hsiu called him "The Man Who Knows Words."

XLII. Another son, of course. He seems to have lost all his family. Here begin several poems of loss. Although they echo the Emperor Wu of Han and many others they are none the less poignant and remind me of the later sepulchral epigrams of the Greek Anthology.

OU YANG HSIU (1007-1072) was one of the most famous writers of the Sung Dynasty and a powerful politician. He held many high offices, among them, Vice-Minister of Rites and Minister of War. He was an early patron of both Su Tung P'o and the reformer, Wang An Shih. Leader of the opposition to Wang An Shih, he retired from all office when the latter came to power. He was one of the creators of the style we think of as characteristically Sung. Waley has translated his "Autumn," the first great *fu* or prose poem in the Sung style. At his best Ou Yang Hsiu is deeply personal, sonorous, and melancholy. He was one of the Sung prose masters, too, and the author of a history of the T'ang Dynasty.

L. There is a famous painting of this poem, many times imitated, to be found in most books of Chinese art.

LI. This was some government office, perhaps the Post Office.

LIII. These poems cannot be appreciated fully unless it is realized that East Wind, plum blossoms, warm mist, and so forth, are mild sexual symbols. Ou Yang Hsiu is a master, along with other virtues, of a quiet eroticism, dreamy as a Sung painting of plum blossoms in mist.

LIV. This is a scarcely veiled description of a sexual encounter, the postcoital *tristia* of Latin poetry.

LV. An ambiguous poem like this foreshadows thousands of Japanese verses.

LVI. The absent friend is Mei Yao Ch'en. "Aware of the music of verse," literally, "the Shao music," which so entranced Confucius he could not eat meat for three months. A lot of nonsense, following the classic authors, is written about the disappearance of the ancient music in the "burning of books"—the musical idiom of a people is extraordinarily resistant to change.

SU TUNG P'O (1036-1101) named Su Shih, belonged to a powerful family of officials and scholars. Under the protection of his father's patron, Ou Yang Hsiu, he rose to prominence when very young. At first he held various provincial posts. Shortly after he was called to office he came into conflict with the famous reformer, Wang An Shih. I should explain that the early years of Sung witnessed a tremendous increase in trade and rise in the general standard of living. Wang proposed to stem this rising tide of commercialism with a series of economic measures which returned all power to the central authority and curbed, in fact attempted to abolish, the mercantile classes and reform the agricultural system. It has been called, with little accuracy, a program of state socialism and autarchy. Actually it was the purest "Neo Confucianism" of a kind different from that which, as a philosophy, later got the name. But the scholar gentry—the Confucianists—were violently opposed. Wang An Shih was simply too unconventional for them. However, for a time, under a new emperor, his schemes were put into effect, with doubtful results. As one of Wang's leading opponents Su Tung P'o then entered upon a period of remarkable vicissitude. He first was moved out of the court to the governorship of Hangchow and then exiled altogether, once as far away as Hainan. His life was a series of ups and downs—out to exile, back to court, back to exile again. He even spent three months in prison. He seems to have been a good, conventional administrator, loved by the people under him but arrogant and rash with equals or supervisors. He was also an excellent painter; his ink paintings of bamboos are superlative. They are imitated to this day and crude forgeries can be found in curio shops. As a painter and something of an esthetician he is one of the founders of the Southern Sung style, one of the glories of Far Eastern culture. He is certainly one of the ten greatest Chinese poets. His work may be full of quotations and allusions to T'ang poetry, T'ao Ch'ien and the classics, but it is still intensely personal and is the climax of early Sung subjectivity. His world is not Tu Fu's. Where the latter sees definite particulars, clear moral issues, bright sharp images, Su Tung P'o's vision is clouded with the all-dissolving systematic doubt of Buddhism and the nihilism of revived philosophical Taoism. It is a less precise world, but a vaster one, and more like our own.

LX. Su wrote several poems and prose poems on this subject. Two will be found in Cyril Drummond Le Gros Clark's *The Prose Poetry of Su Tung P'o*. The cliff was very famous. It was supposed to have been reddened by the fireboats which destroyed the river navy of Ts'ao Ts'ao, the villain of *The Romance of the Three Kingdoms*. The episode is a great favorite in the Chinese theater.

LXI. The Scots call this flicker of herring "keething." The scene is the mouth of the Yangtse.

LXII. "Milk"—actually congee, rice soup. Su lost both his son and his wife (usually, for no reason except Chinese caste, called his mistress), Chao Yun, a girl of remarkable culture, and never recovered from the blow. He is one of the few Chinese poets whose marriage was a love match with an educated member of what used to be called the demimonde. It is significant and unusual that his mother, though a respectable woman, was a woman of education and taste. Su may have also helped to develop the young Li Ch'ing Chao: he was her father's intimate friend.

LXIII. I know of few poems which handle so successfully so many dramatic changes of mood. Compare this subjectivity with Tu Fu's. "Overlooking the Desert" (XVII).

LXIV. I have put as epigraph a verse of the song echoed by Su.

LXVI. Su means that he himself as an official is part of the system of injustice.

LXVIII. Joined swallows, flying with one wing in common, are a symbol of steadfast love.

LXIX. This is a political allegory, as is the next poem. The scholar gentry were always railing against the eunuchs. Their relations with the Emperor were obviously less ceremonial, more personal. Commoners and outlanders, they were often less parochial than the literati and usually did more good than harm.

LXXIII. The dreamy cities and hill-fringed lakes of Wu, portrayed in countless paintings and sung in innumerable poems, were the very heart of Sung civilization, especially after the loss of North China. Nothing has ever been like it in the West, except possibly Tiepolo's Venice, or somnambulist Paris from the Commune to August, 1914. Su was twice governor of Hangchow.

LXXVII. This is a ceremonial washing shortly after birth.

LXXIX. This is the standard interpretation of Su's most famous short poem.

Possibly it is popular because it could just as well mean:

Painted Flower

In the soft East Wind
Rising moonbeams float
On mingled mist and incense.
The moon spies on us
Over the edge of the balcony.
The girl I have hired
Falls asleep. Pensively
I hold up a gilded candle
And look long at her painted beauty.

I like to think of this as written at the first encounter with the girl who was long his lover—Su Hsiao-Hsiao, the famous courtesan whose tomb is still venerated beside the West Lake at Hangchow.

LXXXII. The resemblance to Francis Jammes is startling.

LI CH'ING CHAO (1081-1140) belongs in the great company of Gaspara Stampa and Louise Labé. Although the poems sound like "abandoned love" because they take off from the standard set piece, "The Deserted Concubine" (as in Li Po's "The Jeweled Stairs Grievance," translated by Pound), they are actually truly personal, written after the death of her husband. Her father was a friend of Su Tung P'o. She is China's greatest poetess, of any period.

LXXXIX. Orchid boats are floating pleasure houses. This poem is packed with echoes.

XC. The Day of Cold Food is a festival of new fire, like the Roman Catholic Holy Saturday.

XCI. Presumably, the pepper plants, now withering, survived from the New Year.

Lu Yu (1125-1209) is the least classical of the major Sung poets. Although a member of the scholar gentry he never attained, or desired, high office, and seems to have been genuinely far from rich, especially toward the end of his life. Understand that throughout China's history a real "poor farmer" never got a chance to read or write anything. His poetry is loose, casual. It should be—he wrote about eleven thousand poems. For this reason, perhaps, his best poems have that easy directness that is supposed to come only with rare concentrated effort. By his day Sung China had retreated to the South and the Golden Tartars in the North were already being threatened by the Mongols who were soon to overwhelm all. Lu Yu's patriotism was not prepared to accept the modus vivendi less doctrinaire minds had worked out and his stirring agitational poems against the invader have been very popular in twentieth century China where everybody has been an invader to everybody else.

XCII. There is a veiled ironic reference to a Sung Buddhist saint who was reputed to live only on honey.

XCIII. Lu speaks in the role of a woman. The poem is a very convincing imitation of the later Sung treatment of the abandoned courtesan set piece, but actually it is an exercise in literary criticism.

XCIV. He refers to Chuang Tsu who was never sure afterwards he wasn't a butterfly dreaming he was a man.

C. Shun and Yu were emperors, Kuei Lung a contentious minister of China's legendary history, supposedly about 2200 B. C.

CI. The reference is to a famous battle in the *Three Kingdoms*.

Chu Hsi (1130-1200) is the great philosopher and historian, founder of Sung Neo-Confucianism. That is, he gave the ancient code of the scholar gentry a new religious and philosophical content, owing much to Ch'an Buddhism (Zen) and Taoism—the sort of etherialization undergone by a doctrine when it no longer corresponds to reality at all. However, he gave Confucianism another 700 years of life. As might be expected, his poetry is formal—"neo-classical."

Hsu Chao (c. 1200)

Chu Shu Chen (c. 1200). Nothing definite is known of her. Soulié de Morant says she was a niece of Chu Hsi. Giles places her in the ninth century, an impossible date for this kind of poetry. Note how much more abandoned she is than even Li Ch'ing Chao.

CXI. "Folded quilt"—habitually sleeping alone.

CXII. Plum blossoms for sexual intercourse.

I have "translated out" or paraphrased many Chinese historical and literary references. I wish these to stand as self-sufficient English poems and have tried to avoid too much exoticism. In fact, I do not consider these notes at all necessary. They just seem to be the custom. At the suggestion of the publisher I have given my own titles, as simple as possible, to poems untitled in Chinese.

New Directions Paperbooks—A Partial Listing

For a complete listing request a free catalog from
New Directions, 80 Eighth Avenue, New York 10011

†Bilingual

**For a complete listing request a free catalog from
New Directions, 80 Eighth Avenue, New York 10011**   †Bilingual